50 Vanilla Chocolate Recipes

By: Kelly Johnson

Table of Contents

- Vanilla Bean Cheesecake
- Chocolate Lava Cake
- Vanilla Cupcakes with Chocolate Frosting
- Chocolate-Dipped Vanilla Biscotti
- Vanilla Chocolate Chip Cookies
- Chocolate Mousse
- Vanilla Panna Cotta with Chocolate Sauce
- Chocolate Vanilla Swirl Cake
- Vanilla Bean Ice Cream
- Chocolate Truffles
- Vanilla Milkshake with Chocolate Syrup
- Chocolate Croissants
- Vanilla Bean Macarons
- Chocolate Vanilla Marble Brownies
- Chocolate-Covered Vanilla Creams
- Vanilla Bean Pudding with Chocolate Shavings
- Chocolate-Covered Vanilla Almonds
- Chocolate Ganache Tart with Vanilla Crust
- Vanilla Cream Filled Chocolates
- Chocolate Vanilla Fudge
- Vanilla Churros with Chocolate Sauce
- Chocolate Eclairs with Vanilla Cream
- Vanilla Ice Cream Sundae with Chocolate Drizzle
- Chocolate-Peanut Butter-Vanilla Layer Bars
- Vanilla Chocolate Chip Pancakes
- Chocolate Vanilla Swirl Cookies
- Vanilla and Chocolate Cake Pops
- Chocolate-Swirled Vanilla Cheesecake Bars
- Vanilla Creme Brulee with Chocolate Garnish
- Chocolate Vanilla Meringues
- Vanilla and Chocolate Rice Krispies Treats
- Chocolate Vanilla Pudding Parfaits
- Chocolate-Covered Vanilla Pretzels
- Vanilla Chocolate Banana Bread
- Chocolate-Covered Vanilla Bean Popsicles

- Vanilla Ice Cream Sandwiches with Chocolate Chips
- Chocolate and Vanilla Milk Chocolate Bars
- Vanilla Chocolate Waffles
- Chocolate-Dipped Vanilla Marshmallows
- Chocolate Vanilla Swirl Pie
- Vanilla Frosting with Chocolate Sprinkles
- Chocolate Vanilla Smoothie
- Vanilla Chocolate Chia Pudding
- Vanilla Chocolate Frappe
- Chocolate-Dipped Vanilla Caramels
- Vanilla Bean Cupcakes with Chocolate Ganache
- Chocolate Vanilla Rice Pudding
- Chocolate-Vanilla Donuts
- Chocolate Vanilla Trifle
- Vanilla Bean Chocolate Chip Scones

Vanilla Bean Cheesecake

Ingredients:

- 1 1/2 cups graham cracker crumbs
- 1/4 cup sugar
- 1/2 cup butter, melted
- 4 (8 oz) packages cream cheese, softened
- 1 cup sugar
- 4 large eggs
- 2 tbsp vanilla bean paste or vanilla extract
- 1 cup sour cream
- 1/4 cup heavy cream

Instructions:

1. Preheat oven to 325°F (163°C).
2. Mix graham cracker crumbs, sugar, and melted butter, then press into the bottom of a springform pan.
3. Beat cream cheese and sugar until smooth. Add eggs one at a time, mixing well after each. Stir in vanilla bean paste.
4. Pour the mixture into the crust and bake for 50-60 minutes until set.
5. Let the cheesecake cool, then refrigerate for 4 hours.
6. Before serving, top with sour cream and heavy cream mixture.

Chocolate Lava Cake

Ingredients:

- 4 oz semi-sweet chocolate
- 1/2 cup butter
- 1 cup powdered sugar
- 2 large eggs
- 2 egg yolks
- 1/2 tsp vanilla extract
- 1/4 cup all-purpose flour
- Pinch of salt

Instructions:

1. Preheat oven to 425°F (220°C).
2. Grease and flour 4 ramekins.
3. Melt chocolate and butter together. Stir in powdered sugar, eggs, egg yolks, vanilla, flour, and salt.
4. Pour batter into ramekins, leaving room for the center to remain soft.
5. Bake for 12-14 minutes until the edges are set but the center is still gooey.
6. Let cool for 1 minute before inverting onto plates. Serve immediately.

Vanilla Cupcakes with Chocolate Frosting

Ingredients for Cupcakes:

- 1 1/2 cups all-purpose flour
- 1 1/2 tsp baking powder
- 1/2 tsp salt
- 1/2 cup unsalted butter, softened
- 1 cup sugar
- 2 large eggs
- 2 tsp vanilla extract
- 1/2 cup milk

Ingredients for Frosting:

- 1/2 cup unsalted butter, softened
- 1 1/2 cups powdered sugar
- 1/4 cup unsweetened cocoa powder
- 1/4 cup milk
- 1 tsp vanilla extract

Instructions:

1. Preheat oven to 350°F (175°C). Line a muffin tin with paper liners.
2. In a bowl, whisk flour, baking powder, and salt. In another, beat butter and sugar until creamy. Add eggs and vanilla, then milk.
3. Mix dry ingredients into wet ingredients until combined.
4. Fill cupcake liners 2/3 full and bake for 18-20 minutes. Let cool completely.
5. For frosting, beat butter and powdered sugar. Add cocoa, milk, and vanilla. Frost cupcakes when cooled.

Chocolate-Dipped Vanilla Biscotti

Ingredients:

- 1 1/2 cups all-purpose flour
- 1 tsp baking powder
- 1/4 tsp salt
- 1/2 cup sugar
- 2 large eggs
- 1 tsp vanilla extract
- 1/2 cup semisweet chocolate, melted

Instructions:

1. Preheat oven to 350°F (175°C). Line a baking sheet with parchment paper.
2. Whisk flour, baking powder, and salt. Beat eggs and sugar, then stir in vanilla. Gradually add dry ingredients.
3. Shape dough into a log and bake for 25-30 minutes until golden.
4. Cool slightly, slice into 1-inch pieces, and bake again for 10-12 minutes.
5. Dip the cooled biscotti into melted chocolate and let set.

Vanilla Chocolate Chip Cookies

Ingredients:

- 1 cup unsalted butter, softened
- 3/4 cup sugar
- 3/4 cup brown sugar
- 2 large eggs
- 2 tsp vanilla extract
- 2 1/4 cups all-purpose flour
- 1 tsp baking soda
- 1/2 tsp salt
- 2 cups chocolate chips

Instructions:

1. Preheat oven to 350°F (175°C). Line baking sheets with parchment paper.
2. Beat butter, sugars, eggs, and vanilla until creamy. Mix in flour, baking soda, and salt.
3. Fold in chocolate chips.
4. Drop dough by spoonfuls onto baking sheets and bake for 10-12 minutes until golden. Let cool on a wire rack.

Chocolate Mousse

Ingredients:

- 4 oz dark chocolate, chopped
- 1 cup heavy cream
- 1 tbsp sugar
- 1 tsp vanilla extract

Instructions:

1. Melt chocolate in a heatproof bowl over simmering water. Let cool slightly.
2. Whip heavy cream with sugar until stiff peaks form.
3. Gently fold in the melted chocolate and vanilla extract.
4. Spoon into serving dishes and refrigerate for 2-3 hours. Serve chilled.

Vanilla Panna Cotta with Chocolate Sauce

Ingredients for Panna Cotta:

- 2 cups heavy cream
- 1 cup milk
- 1/2 cup sugar
- 1 tbsp vanilla extract
- 2 1/2 tsp unflavored gelatin

Ingredients for Chocolate Sauce:

- 1/2 cup heavy cream
- 1/4 cup sugar
- 1/4 cup unsweetened cocoa powder

Instructions:

1. In a saucepan, heat cream, milk, and sugar until sugar dissolves. Stir in vanilla.
2. In a separate bowl, dissolve gelatin in a little water, then add to the cream mixture.
3. Pour into molds and refrigerate for 4 hours.
4. For sauce, whisk together cream, sugar, and cocoa in a saucepan. Heat until smooth.
5. Serve panna cotta with chocolate sauce.

Chocolate Vanilla Swirl Cake

Ingredients:

- 1 1/2 cups all-purpose flour
- 1 tsp baking powder
- 1/2 tsp salt
- 1/2 cup unsalted butter, softened
- 1 cup sugar
- 3 large eggs
- 1 tsp vanilla extract
- 1/2 cup unsweetened cocoa powder
- 1/2 cup milk

Instructions:

1. Preheat oven to 350°F (175°C). Grease and flour a cake pan.
2. Mix flour, baking powder, and salt. Beat butter and sugar, then add eggs and vanilla.
3. Divide batter in half. Stir cocoa powder into one portion, and leave the other plain.
4. Alternately spoon vanilla and chocolate batters into the pan. Swirl with a knife.
5. Bake for 25-30 minutes. Cool before serving.

Vanilla Bean Ice Cream

Ingredients:

- 2 cups heavy cream
- 1 cup whole milk
- 3/4 cup sugar
- 1 vanilla bean, split and scraped (or 2 tsp vanilla extract)
- 4 large egg yolks

Instructions:

1. Heat cream, milk, sugar, and vanilla bean in a saucepan until warm.
2. In a separate bowl, whisk egg yolks. Slowly add the warm cream mixture, then return to the saucepan.
3. Cook over low heat, stirring until thickened. Cool completely.
4. Pour into an ice cream maker and churn according to the manufacturer's instructions.

Chocolate Truffles

Ingredients:

- 8 oz semisweet chocolate, chopped
- 1/2 cup heavy cream
- 1 tsp vanilla extract
- Cocoa powder, crushed nuts, or sprinkles for coating

Instructions:

1. Heat cream until simmering, then pour over chopped chocolate. Stir until smooth.
2. Add vanilla extract and chill the mixture for 1-2 hours.
3. Roll into balls and coat with cocoa powder, nuts, or sprinkles.
4. Refrigerate until firm, then serve.

Vanilla Milkshake with Chocolate Syrup

Ingredients:

- 2 cups vanilla ice cream
- 1 cup milk
- 1 tsp vanilla extract
- 2 tbsp chocolate syrup
- Whipped cream for topping (optional)

Instructions:

1. Blend vanilla ice cream, milk, and vanilla extract until smooth.
2. Drizzle chocolate syrup inside a glass.
3. Pour the milkshake into the glass and top with whipped cream, if desired.
4. Serve with extra chocolate syrup for drizzling.

Chocolate Croissants

Ingredients:

- 1 sheet puff pastry
- 2 oz dark chocolate or chocolate chips
- 1 egg, beaten (for egg wash)
- 1 tbsp sugar (optional)

Instructions:

1. Preheat oven to 400°F (200°C).
2. Roll out the puff pastry and cut it into triangles.
3. Place a small piece of chocolate at the base of each triangle.
4. Roll up the triangles into croissant shapes and brush with beaten egg.
5. Bake for 15-18 minutes until golden brown, then dust with sugar if desired.

Vanilla Bean Macarons

Ingredients for Shells:

- 1 cup powdered sugar
- 1/2 cup almond flour
- 2 large egg whites
- 1/4 cup granulated sugar
- 1 tsp vanilla bean paste

Ingredients for Filling:

- 1/2 cup butter, softened
- 1 1/2 cups powdered sugar
- 1 tsp vanilla extract
- 2 tbsp heavy cream

Instructions:

1. Preheat oven to 300°F (150°C) and line a baking sheet with parchment paper.
2. Sift powdered sugar and almond flour together.
3. Whip egg whites until soft peaks form, then add granulated sugar and whip until stiff peaks.
4. Gently fold the dry ingredients into the egg whites.
5. Pipe the batter onto the baking sheet in small circles.
6. Let the macarons rest for 30-60 minutes, then bake for 18-20 minutes.
7. For the filling, beat butter, powdered sugar, vanilla, and heavy cream until smooth.
8. Sandwich the shells with the filling.

Chocolate Vanilla Marble Brownies

Ingredients:

- 1 box brownie mix (or homemade brownie recipe)
- 1/2 cup vanilla batter (from brownie mix or recipe)
- 1/2 cup chocolate batter (from brownie mix or recipe)
- 1/4 cup chocolate chips (optional)

Instructions:

1. Preheat oven to the temperature specified on the brownie mix package.
2. Prepare brownie batter as directed, then divide it into two bowls.
3. Add vanilla extract to one bowl and mix well.
4. Layer both batters in a baking pan, then swirl together with a knife.
5. Bake according to package directions, adding chocolate chips if desired.

Chocolate-Covered Vanilla Creams

Ingredients:

- 1 package vanilla wafer cookies
- 1/2 cup powdered sugar
- 1/4 cup butter, softened
- 1 tsp vanilla extract
- 6 oz dark chocolate, melted

Instructions:

1. Beat together powdered sugar, butter, and vanilla extract until smooth.
2. Spread a small amount of the cream mixture onto each wafer cookie.
3. Dip the filled cookies into melted chocolate and place on wax paper to set.
4. Chill in the fridge for 30 minutes.

Vanilla Bean Pudding with Chocolate Shavings

Ingredients:

- 2 cups whole milk
- 1/2 cup sugar
- 1 tbsp cornstarch
- 1 tsp vanilla bean paste
- 1/4 cup dark chocolate, shaved

Instructions:

1. In a saucepan, whisk milk, sugar, and cornstarch. Cook over medium heat until thickened.
2. Stir in vanilla bean paste.
3. Pour into serving dishes and refrigerate for 2-3 hours.
4. Top with chocolate shavings before serving.

Chocolate-Covered Vanilla Almonds

Ingredients:

- 1 cup whole almonds
- 4 oz dark chocolate, melted
- 1 tsp vanilla extract

Instructions:

1. Toast almonds in a pan over low heat for 5-7 minutes.
2. Dip almonds into melted chocolate, then place on a baking sheet lined with parchment paper.
3. Drizzle with vanilla extract.
4. Chill in the fridge for 20-30 minutes until set.

Chocolate Ganache Tart with Vanilla Crust

Ingredients for Crust:

- 1 1/2 cups graham cracker crumbs
- 1/4 cup sugar
- 1/2 cup butter, melted

Ingredients for Ganache:

- 8 oz dark chocolate, chopped
- 1 cup heavy cream
- 1 tsp vanilla extract

Instructions:

1. Preheat oven to 350°F (175°C).
2. Mix graham cracker crumbs, sugar, and melted butter. Press into the base of a tart pan.
3. Bake for 10-12 minutes and cool.
4. For the ganache, heat heavy cream in a saucepan until simmering, then pour over chopped chocolate. Stir until smooth.
5. Stir in vanilla extract and pour into the cooled crust.
6. Refrigerate for 2-3 hours until set.

Vanilla Cream Filled Chocolates

Ingredients for Filling:

- 1/2 cup heavy cream
- 2 tbsp butter
- 1 cup powdered sugar
- 1 tsp vanilla extract

Ingredients for Chocolate Coating:

- 8 oz dark chocolate, melted

Instructions:

1. Heat heavy cream and butter until melted.
2. Stir in powdered sugar and vanilla extract, then refrigerate until firm.
3. Roll the cream mixture into small balls.
4. Dip into melted chocolate and set on wax paper.
5. Refrigerate for 30 minutes until the chocolate hardens.

Chocolate Vanilla Fudge

Ingredients:

- 1/2 cup butter
- 1 cup heavy cream
- 2 cups sugar
- 1/2 cup unsweetened cocoa powder
- 1 tsp vanilla extract
- 1/2 cup white chocolate chips

Instructions:

1. In a saucepan, melt butter and cream over medium heat.
2. Stir in sugar and cocoa powder, and bring to a boil.
3. Reduce heat and cook for 5-7 minutes.
4. Stir in vanilla extract and white chocolate chips.
5. Pour into a greased pan and refrigerate until set.

Vanilla Churros with Chocolate Sauce

Ingredients for Churros:

- 1 cup water
- 2 tbsp butter
- 1 tsp vanilla extract
- 1 cup all-purpose flour
- 1/4 tsp salt
- 2 eggs
- 1/2 cup sugar (for coating)
- 1 tsp cinnamon (for coating)

Ingredients for Chocolate Sauce:

- 4 oz dark chocolate, chopped
- 1/2 cup heavy cream

Instructions:

1. In a saucepan, bring water, butter, and vanilla to a boil.
2. Stir in flour and salt until smooth, then let cool slightly.
3. Add eggs one at a time, mixing well.
4. Heat oil in a pan and fry churros until golden.
5. Combine sugar and cinnamon in a bowl and roll churros in it.
6. For the sauce, heat heavy cream and pour over chopped chocolate. Stir until smooth.
7. Serve churros with chocolate sauce for dipping.

Chocolate Eclairs with Vanilla Cream

Ingredients for Eclairs:

- 1 cup water
- 1/2 cup unsalted butter
- 1 cup all-purpose flour
- 4 large eggs
- 1 tsp vanilla extract

Ingredients for Vanilla Cream Filling:

- 2 cups heavy cream
- 1/2 cup sugar
- 2 tsp vanilla extract
- 2 tbsp cornstarch

Ingredients for Chocolate Glaze:

- 4 oz dark chocolate, chopped
- 1/2 cup heavy cream

Instructions:

1. Preheat oven to 425°F (220°C).
2. In a saucepan, bring water and butter to a boil, then add flour and stir until smooth.
3. Remove from heat, add eggs one at a time, and stir in vanilla.
4. Pipe the dough onto a baking sheet and bake for 25-30 minutes.
5. For the cream filling, whip heavy cream, sugar, and vanilla until stiff peaks form.
6. For the glaze, heat cream and pour over chopped chocolate; stir until smooth.
7. Slice eclairs open, fill with cream, and drizzle with chocolate glaze.

Vanilla Ice Cream Sundae with Chocolate Drizzle

Ingredients:

- 2 scoops vanilla ice cream
- 2 tbsp chocolate syrup
- 1 tbsp crushed nuts (optional)
- Whipped cream (optional)
- Maraschino cherry (optional)

Instructions:

1. Scoop vanilla ice cream into a bowl or sundae dish.
2. Drizzle chocolate syrup over the ice cream.
3. Top with whipped cream, crushed nuts, and a maraschino cherry, if desired.

Chocolate-Peanut Butter-Vanilla Layer Bars

Ingredients:

- 1 1/2 cups graham cracker crumbs
- 1/2 cup unsalted butter, melted
- 1 cup powdered sugar
- 1/2 cup peanut butter
- 1 cup chocolate chips
- 1/2 cup heavy cream
- 1 tsp vanilla extract

Instructions:

1. Mix graham cracker crumbs, butter, powdered sugar, and peanut butter. Press into a greased pan.
2. Melt chocolate chips and heavy cream together, then stir in vanilla.
3. Pour chocolate over the peanut butter layer and refrigerate for 2 hours.
4. Cut into bars and serve.

Vanilla Chocolate Chip Pancakes

Ingredients:

- 1 cup all-purpose flour
- 2 tbsp sugar
- 1 tbsp baking powder
- 1/2 tsp salt
- 1 large egg
- 3/4 cup milk
- 1 tsp vanilla extract
- 1/4 cup chocolate chips

Instructions:

1. Whisk together flour, sugar, baking powder, and salt.
2. In another bowl, whisk egg, milk, and vanilla extract.
3. Pour wet ingredients into dry ingredients and stir until just combined.
4. Fold in chocolate chips.
5. Heat a non-stick pan over medium heat and cook pancakes, flipping when bubbles form on the surface.
6. Serve with syrup or extra chocolate chips.

Chocolate Vanilla Swirl Cookies

Ingredients:

- 1 cup unsalted butter, softened
- 1 cup sugar
- 2 large eggs
- 2 tsp vanilla extract
- 2 cups all-purpose flour
- 1/2 tsp baking powder
- 1/4 cup unsweetened cocoa powder

Instructions:

1. Preheat oven to 350°F (175°C).
2. Beat butter, sugar, eggs, and vanilla until smooth.
3. Mix flour and baking powder, then gradually add to the butter mixture.
4. Divide dough in half, mixing cocoa powder into one half.
5. Roll out both doughs, then swirl them together.
6. Shape into cookies and bake for 10-12 minutes.

Vanilla and Chocolate Cake Pops

Ingredients:

- 1 box vanilla cake mix
- 1 box chocolate cake mix
- 1 cup frosting (store-bought or homemade)
- 8 oz dark chocolate, melted
- Sprinkles (optional)

Instructions:

1. Bake vanilla and chocolate cakes according to package directions.
2. Crumble cakes into crumbs and mix with frosting.
3. Roll mixture into small balls and insert cake pop sticks.
4. Dip in melted chocolate and decorate with sprinkles.
5. Chill until set.

Chocolate-Swirled Vanilla Cheesecake Bars

Ingredients for Crust:

- 1 1/2 cups graham cracker crumbs
- 1/4 cup sugar
- 1/2 cup butter, melted

Ingredients for Filling:

- 2 cups cream cheese, softened
- 1 cup sugar
- 2 tsp vanilla extract
- 2 large eggs
- 1/4 cup unsweetened cocoa powder

Instructions:

1. Preheat oven to 325°F (163°C).
2. Combine graham cracker crumbs, sugar, and butter, then press into the bottom of a pan.
3. Beat cream cheese, sugar, and vanilla until smooth. Add eggs one at a time.
4. Divide batter in half. Mix cocoa powder into one half, then swirl it with the vanilla batter.
5. Bake for 25-30 minutes, then cool and refrigerate for 2 hours.

Vanilla Creme Brulee with Chocolate Garnish

Ingredients:

- 2 cups heavy cream
- 1 vanilla bean, split
- 5 large egg yolks
- 1/2 cup sugar
- 2 tbsp cocoa powder (for garnish)

Instructions:

1. Preheat oven to 325°F (163°C).
2. Heat cream and vanilla bean in a saucepan, then remove from heat and let steep for 10 minutes.
3. Whisk egg yolks and sugar until pale. Slowly add cream mixture.
4. Pour into ramekins and bake for 30-35 minutes.
5. Let cool and refrigerate. Before serving, dust with cocoa powder.

Chocolate Vanilla Meringues

Ingredients:

- 4 large egg whites
- 1 cup sugar
- 1/2 tsp vanilla extract
- 1 tbsp unsweetened cocoa powder

Instructions:

1. Preheat oven to 225°F (110°C).
2. Beat egg whites until stiff peaks form. Gradually add sugar and vanilla.
3. Fold in cocoa powder.
4. Spoon meringue onto a baking sheet and bake for 1 hour. Let cool completely.

Vanilla and Chocolate Rice Krispies Treats

Ingredients for Vanilla Layer:

- 3 cups Rice Krispies cereal
- 2 tbsp butter
- 1 1/2 cups marshmallows

Ingredients for Chocolate Layer:

- 3 cups Rice Krispies cereal
- 2 tbsp butter
- 1 1/2 cups marshmallows
- 1/2 cup chocolate chips

Instructions:

1. Melt butter and marshmallows for the vanilla layer. Stir in Rice Krispies and press into a pan.
2. Repeat for the chocolate layer, adding chocolate chips to the melted marshmallow mixture.
3. Layer the chocolate on top of the vanilla, then refrigerate until set.

Chocolate Vanilla Pudding Parfaits

Ingredients for Pudding:

- 2 cups milk
- 1/2 cup sugar
- 2 tbsp cornstarch
- 1 tsp vanilla extract
- 2 tbsp unsweetened cocoa powder

Instructions:

1. Whisk together milk, sugar, cornstarch, and cocoa powder in a saucepan.
2. Cook over medium heat until thickened. Remove from heat and stir in vanilla.
3. Layer chocolate and vanilla pudding in glasses and refrigerate for 2-3 hours before serving.

Chocolate-Covered Vanilla Pretzels

Ingredients:

- 12 pretzels
- 4 oz white chocolate, melted
- 4 oz dark chocolate, melted
- Sprinkles (optional)

Instructions:

1. Dip pretzels into white chocolate, then into dark chocolate for a swirled effect.
2. Place on parchment paper and refrigerate until set.
3. Optionally, decorate with sprinkles before chilling.

Vanilla Chocolate Banana Bread

Ingredients:

- 2 ripe bananas, mashed
- 2 cups all-purpose flour
- 1 tsp baking soda
- 1/4 tsp salt
- 1/2 cup sugar
- 1/4 cup butter, softened
- 2 large eggs
- 1 tsp vanilla extract
- 1/4 cup cocoa powder
- 1/2 cup chocolate chips

Instructions:

1. Preheat oven to 350°F (175°C).
2. In a bowl, mix flour, baking soda, and salt.
3. In another bowl, beat sugar, butter, eggs, and vanilla. Stir in mashed bananas.
4. Fold in dry ingredients until just combined.
5. Divide batter into two bowls. In one, stir in cocoa powder.
6. Layer the two batters in a loaf pan and swirl together.
7. Bake for 60-70 minutes or until a toothpick comes out clean.

Chocolate-Covered Vanilla Bean Popsicles

Ingredients:

- 1 cup heavy cream
- 1 cup milk
- 1/4 cup sugar
- 1 vanilla bean, scraped
- 4 oz dark chocolate, melted

Instructions:

1. Whisk together heavy cream, milk, sugar, and vanilla bean seeds in a bowl.
2. Pour mixture into popsicle molds and freeze for 4-6 hours.
3. Once frozen, dip popsicles into melted dark chocolate and freeze again for 15 minutes.

Vanilla Ice Cream Sandwiches with Chocolate Chips

Ingredients for Cookies:

- 1 1/2 cups all-purpose flour
- 1 tsp baking soda
- 1/2 tsp salt
- 1/2 cup butter, softened
- 1/2 cup sugar
- 1/2 cup brown sugar
- 1 tsp vanilla extract
- 1 egg
- 1 cup chocolate chips

Ingredients for Ice Cream Filling:

- 2 cups vanilla ice cream

Instructions:

1. Preheat oven to 350°F (175°C).
2. Mix flour, baking soda, and salt.
3. Beat butter, sugar, brown sugar, vanilla, and egg until smooth. Add dry ingredients and chocolate chips.
4. Roll dough into balls and flatten slightly on a baking sheet.
5. Bake for 8-10 minutes. Cool completely.
6. Scoop vanilla ice cream onto one cookie and top with another. Freeze until firm.

Chocolate and Vanilla Milk Chocolate Bars

Ingredients:

- 8 oz dark chocolate, chopped
- 8 oz milk chocolate, chopped
- 1 tsp vanilla extract

Instructions:

1. Melt dark chocolate and milk chocolate in separate bowls over a double boiler.
2. Stir in vanilla extract into the milk chocolate.
3. Layer the dark chocolate and milk chocolate in a mold, swirling to create a marbled effect.
4. Let the chocolate harden in the refrigerator for 2-3 hours.

Vanilla Chocolate Waffles

Ingredients for Waffles:

- 2 cups all-purpose flour
- 2 tsp baking powder
- 1/2 tsp salt
- 1/4 cup sugar
- 2 eggs
- 1 1/2 cups milk
- 1 tsp vanilla extract
- 1/4 cup cocoa powder
- 1/4 cup melted butter

Instructions:

1. Preheat waffle iron.
2. In a bowl, mix flour, baking powder, salt, and sugar.
3. In another bowl, whisk eggs, milk, vanilla, and melted butter.
4. Divide the batter in two, adding cocoa powder to one half.
5. Pour a little of each batter into the waffle iron, swirling them together.
6. Cook according to waffle iron instructions and serve with syrup.

Chocolate-Dipped Vanilla Marshmallows

Ingredients:

- 1 package marshmallows
- 4 oz dark chocolate, melted
- 1 tsp vanilla extract (optional)
- Sprinkles (optional)

Instructions:

1. Insert a toothpick into each marshmallow.
2. Dip each marshmallow into the melted dark chocolate.
3. Place on parchment paper to set.
4. Optionally, drizzle with vanilla extract or decorate with sprinkles.

Chocolate Vanilla Swirl Pie

Ingredients for Crust:

- 1 1/2 cups graham cracker crumbs
- 1/4 cup sugar
- 1/2 cup butter, melted

Ingredients for Filling:

- 8 oz cream cheese, softened
- 1/2 cup sugar
- 1 cup vanilla pudding (prepared)
- 1/4 cup cocoa powder
- 1/2 cup chocolate pudding (prepared)

Instructions:

1. Preheat oven to 350°F (175°C).
2. Mix graham cracker crumbs, sugar, and melted butter, then press into a pie pan.
3. Beat cream cheese and sugar until smooth. Fold in vanilla pudding.
4. Divide filling in half and mix cocoa powder into one half.
5. Layer the vanilla and chocolate filling and swirl together.
6. Bake for 25-30 minutes and cool before serving.

Vanilla Frosting with Chocolate Sprinkles

Ingredients:

- 1 cup butter, softened
- 4 cups powdered sugar
- 1 tsp vanilla extract
- 2-3 tbsp milk
- Chocolate sprinkles

Instructions:

1. Beat butter, powdered sugar, vanilla, and milk until smooth and creamy.
2. Spread frosting on cakes or cupcakes.
3. Sprinkle with chocolate sprinkles and serve.

Chocolate Vanilla Smoothie

Ingredients:

- 1 banana
- 1/2 cup milk
- 1 tbsp cocoa powder
- 1 tsp vanilla extract
- 1/2 cup vanilla yogurt
- Ice cubes

Instructions:

1. Blend all ingredients together until smooth.
2. Serve in a glass and enjoy!

Vanilla Chocolate Chia Pudding

Ingredients:

- 1/2 cup chia seeds
- 2 cups milk
- 1 tbsp honey or maple syrup
- 1 tsp vanilla extract
- 2 tbsp cocoa powder

Instructions:

1. Mix chia seeds, milk, honey, and vanilla extract in a bowl.
2. Divide the mixture in half, adding cocoa powder to one half.
3. Refrigerate for at least 4 hours or overnight.
4. Serve with additional toppings, if desired.

Vanilla Chocolate Frappe

Ingredients:

- 1 cup brewed coffee, cooled
- 1/2 cup milk
- 1/2 cup vanilla ice cream
- 1 tbsp cocoa powder
- 1 tbsp sugar
- Ice cubes
- Whipped cream (optional)

Instructions:

1. In a blender, combine coffee, milk, vanilla ice cream, cocoa powder, sugar, and ice cubes.
2. Blend until smooth and frothy.
3. Pour into a glass and top with whipped cream, if desired.

Chocolate-Dipped Vanilla Caramels

Ingredients:

- 1 1/2 cups sugar
- 1/2 cup unsalted butter
- 1/2 cup heavy cream
- 1/2 tsp vanilla extract
- 4 oz dark chocolate, melted

Instructions:

1. In a saucepan, melt sugar and butter over medium heat until it forms a golden caramel.
2. Stir in heavy cream and vanilla extract, then allow to cool slightly.
3. Pour the caramel into a greased pan and refrigerate until set, about 1 hour.
4. Cut the caramel into squares, then dip in melted chocolate.
5. Let the chocolate set before serving.

Vanilla Bean Cupcakes with Chocolate Ganache

Ingredients for Cupcakes:

- 1 1/2 cups all-purpose flour
- 1 1/2 tsp baking powder
- 1/4 tsp salt
- 1/2 cup butter, softened
- 3/4 cup sugar
- 2 eggs
- 1 tsp vanilla bean paste
- 1/2 cup milk

Ingredients for Ganache:

- 4 oz dark chocolate, chopped
- 1/4 cup heavy cream

Instructions:

1. Preheat oven to 350°F (175°C).
2. Beat butter and sugar until fluffy, then add eggs and vanilla paste.
3. Gradually add flour, baking powder, and salt. Mix in milk.
4. Pour batter into cupcake liners and bake for 18-20 minutes.
5. For the ganache, heat cream in a saucepan, then pour over chopped chocolate. Stir until smooth.
6. Once cupcakes have cooled, top with chocolate ganache.

Chocolate Vanilla Rice Pudding

Ingredients:

- 1/2 cup Arborio rice
- 2 cups milk
- 1/4 cup sugar
- 1/2 tsp vanilla extract
- 1 tbsp cocoa powder
- 1/4 cup chocolate chips (optional)

Instructions:

1. In a saucepan, combine rice, milk, and sugar. Cook over medium heat, stirring often.
2. Once the rice is soft and the mixture thickens, stir in vanilla extract.
3. Divide the mixture into two bowls. Stir cocoa powder into one bowl.
4. Layer the vanilla and chocolate rice pudding in serving cups and top with chocolate chips if desired.

Chocolate-Vanilla Donuts

Ingredients for Donuts:

- 1 1/2 cups all-purpose flour
- 1/2 cup sugar
- 1 1/2 tsp baking powder
- 1/4 tsp salt
- 1/2 cup milk
- 2 eggs
- 1 tsp vanilla extract
- 1/4 cup cocoa powder
- 1/4 cup melted butter

Ingredients for Glaze:

- 1 cup powdered sugar
- 2 tbsp milk
- 1 tsp vanilla extract

Instructions:

1. Preheat oven to 350°F (175°C) and grease a donut pan.
2. In a bowl, mix flour, sugar, baking powder, and salt.
3. In another bowl, whisk eggs, milk, and vanilla extract. Add wet ingredients to dry and mix until combined.
4. Divide batter in half and add cocoa powder to one half.
5. Spoon batters into the donut pan, swirling together for a marble effect.
6. Bake for 12-15 minutes.
7. For the glaze, mix powdered sugar, milk, and vanilla extract. Dip cooled donuts into the glaze.

Chocolate Vanilla Trifle

Ingredients:

- 1 pound chocolate cake, cubed
- 1 pound vanilla cake, cubed
- 1 cup chocolate pudding
- 1 cup vanilla pudding
- 2 cups whipped cream
- Chocolate shavings or sprinkles (optional)

Instructions:

1. In a large trifle dish, layer chocolate cake cubes at the bottom.
2. Top with chocolate pudding, followed by a layer of vanilla cake cubes.
3. Add vanilla pudding, then repeat the layers.
4. Finish with whipped cream and sprinkle with chocolate shavings or sprinkles.
5. Refrigerate for 2-3 hours before serving.

Vanilla Bean Chocolate Chip Scones

Ingredients:

- 2 cups all-purpose flour
- 1/4 cup sugar
- 2 tsp baking powder
- 1/2 tsp salt
- 1/2 cup unsalted butter, cold
- 1/2 cup milk
- 1 egg
- 1 tsp vanilla bean paste
- 1/2 cup chocolate chips

Instructions:

1. Preheat oven to 375°F (190°C).
2. In a bowl, combine flour, sugar, baking powder, and salt.
3. Cut in the cold butter until the mixture resembles coarse crumbs.
4. In another bowl, whisk milk, egg, and vanilla bean paste. Add to the dry ingredients.
5. Gently fold in chocolate chips.
6. Shape dough into a circle and cut into wedges.
7. Bake for 15-20 minutes or until golden.

www.ingramcontent.com/pod-product-compliance
Lightning Source LLC
LaVergne TN
LVHW081507060526
838201LV00056BA/2973